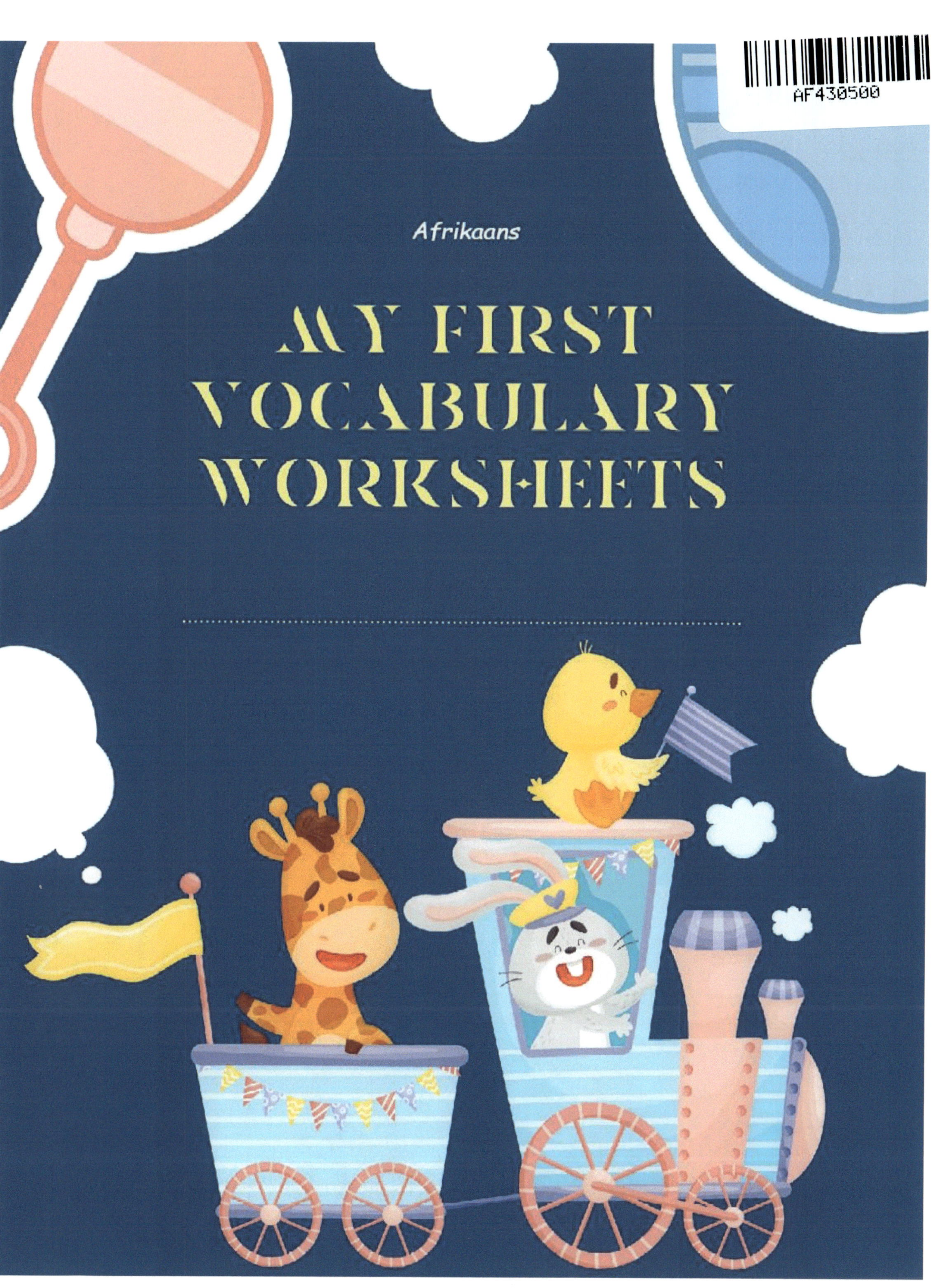
Afrikaans
MY FIRST
VOCABULARY
WORKSHEETS
AF430500

Name : _______________________

Trace the words. Cut out the images at the bottom. Match the words with the images by pasting the images inside the boxes.

baba

paste

mier

paste

vliegtuig

paste

appel

paste

Name : _______________________________

Read, trace, and write the words. Match the images with the traced words by writing the number that is shown on top of each image with the correct word.

bal

bal

Number _______________

piesang

piesang

Number _______________

bad

bad

Number _______________

beer

beer

Number _______________

Name: _______________________ Date: _______________

Today is:

Direction: Read, trace, and write the words.

| 1 | 2 | 3 | 4 |

no.	bed
no.	bee
no.	groot
no.	voël

Name: ____________________ Date: ____________________

Today is: Monday Tuesday Wednesday Thursday Friday

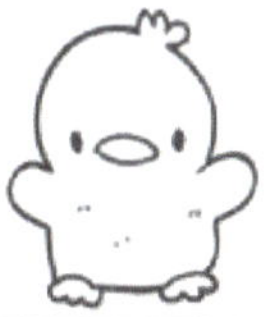

Direction: Read, trace, and write the words.

1	2	3	4
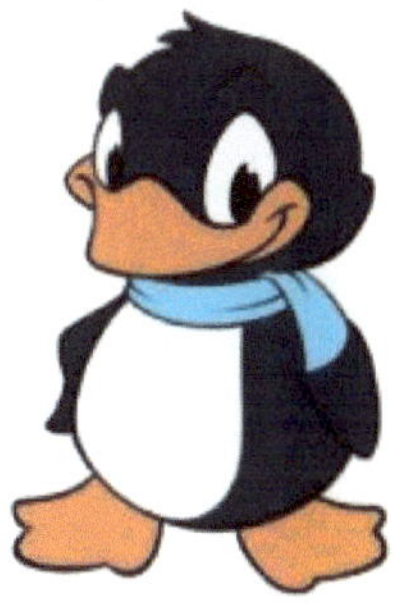	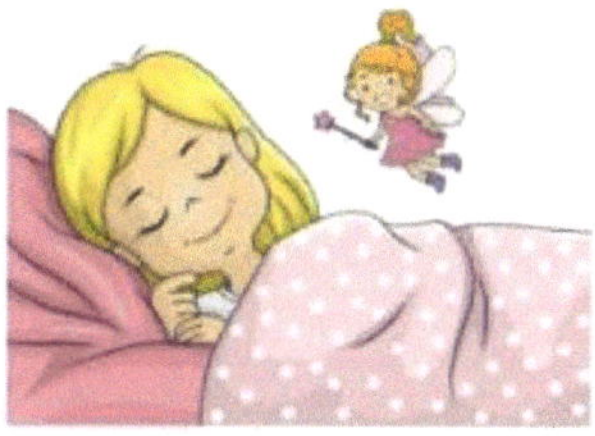	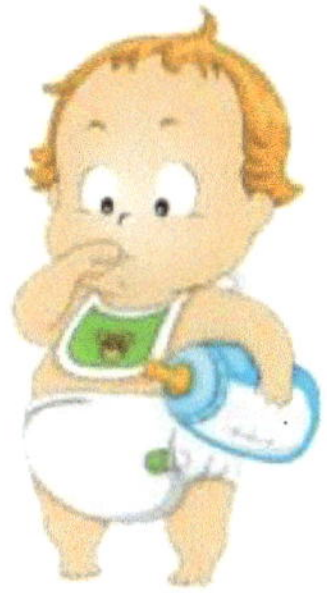	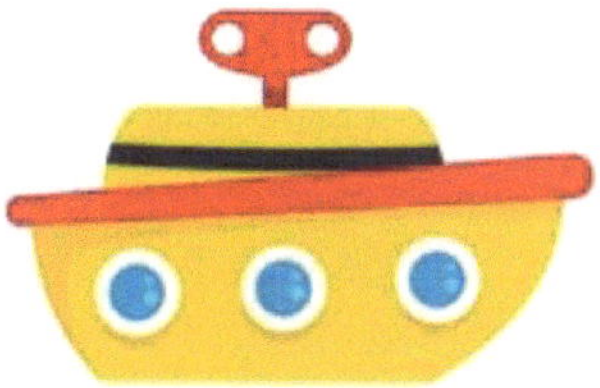

no. ____ kombers

no. ____ swart

no. ____ boot

no. ____ bottel

Name : ______________________

Direction: Match each word to the right picture. Practice writing the word.

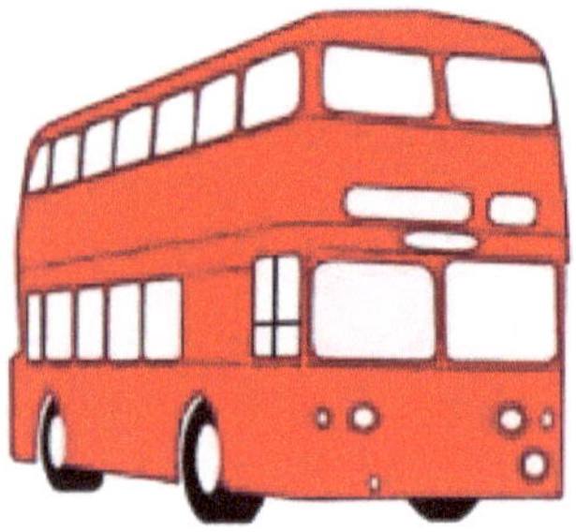

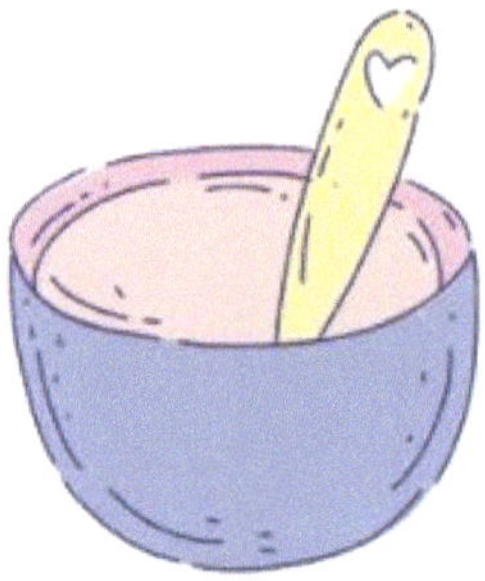

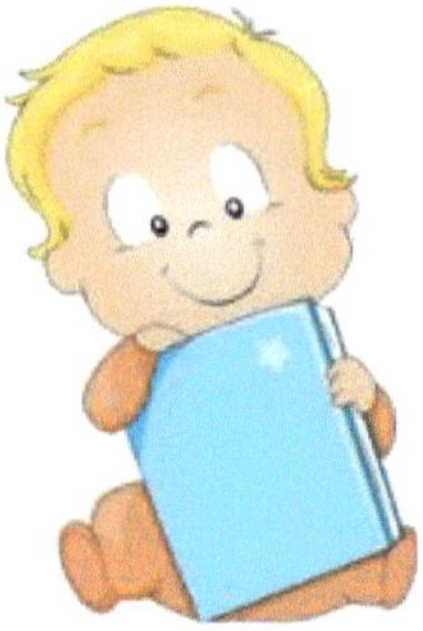

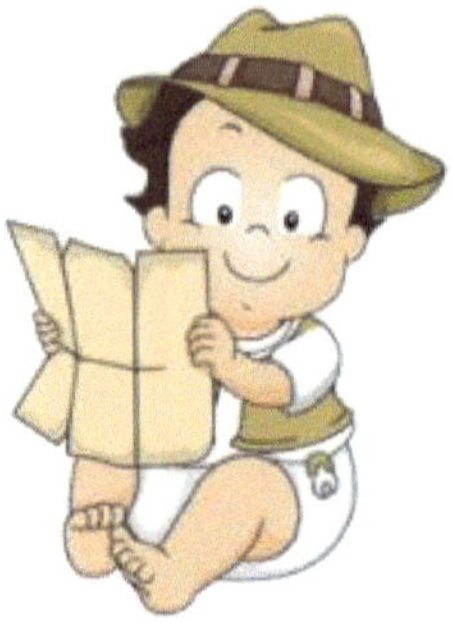

bus

seuntjie

bruin

bak

Spelling Made Easy....

Name : _______________________________

Trace the words. Cut out the images at the bottom. Match the words with the images by pasting the images inside the boxes.

vang

paste

voertuig

paste

kat

paste

koek

paste

Name : ___________________________

Direction: Match each word to the right picture. Practice writing the word.

kinders

klok

kleur

koekie

Name : _______________________________

Direction: Match each word to the right picture. Practice writing the word.

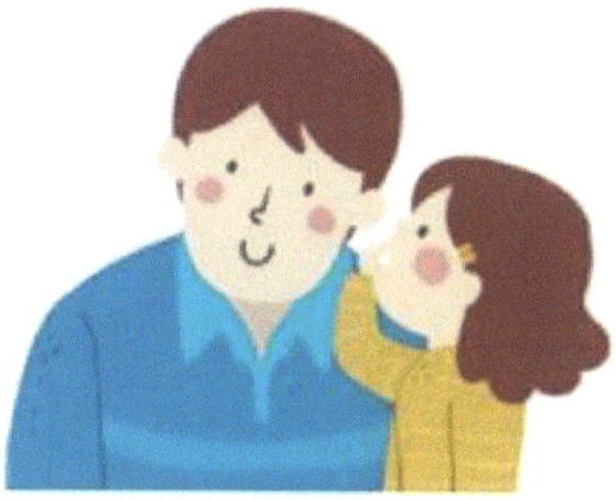

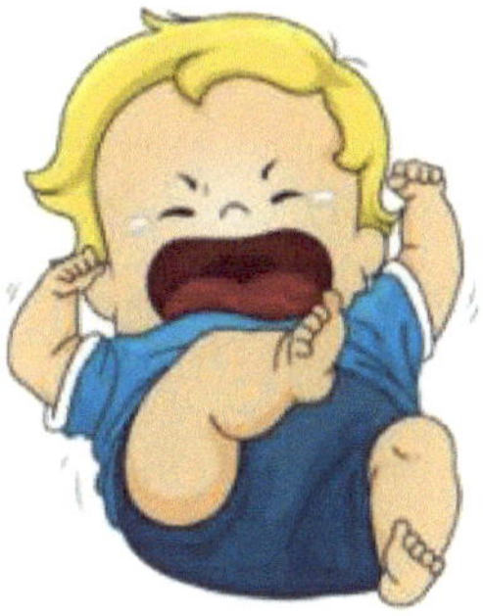

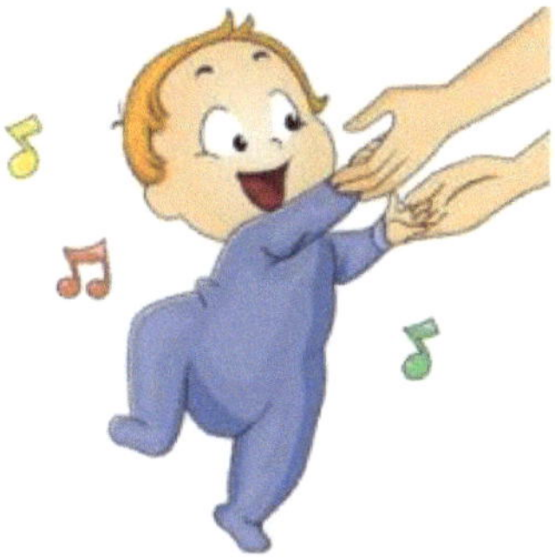

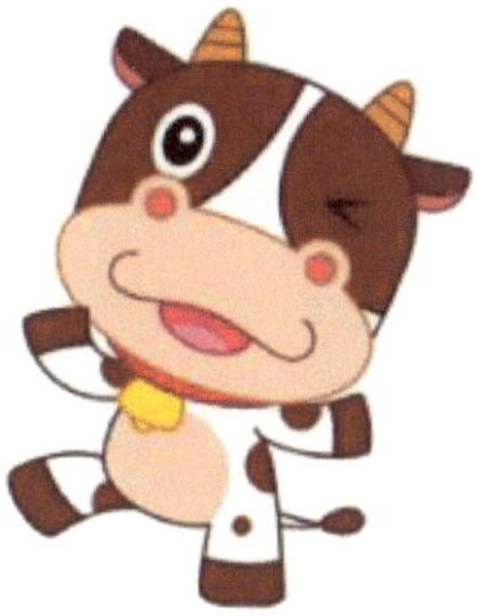

koei

geroep

pa

dans

Name : _______________________________

Read, trace, and write the words. Match the images with the traced words by writing the number that is shown on top of each image with the correct word.

hond

hond

Number _______________

takbokke

takbokke

Number _______________

pop

pop

Number _______________

drink

drink

Number _______________

1

2

3

4

Name : _______________________________

Trace the words. Cut out the images at the bottom. Match the words with the images by pasting the images inside the boxes.

eet

paste

aarde

paste

eend

paste

eier

paste

Name : ___________________________________

Read, trace, and write the words. Match the images with the traced words by writing the number that is shown on top of each image with the correct word.

olifant

olifant

Number ____________

vis

vis

Number ____________

vyf

vyf

Number ____________

vlag

vlag

Number ____________

Name : _______________________________

Trace the words. Cut out the images at the bottom. Match the words with the images by pasting the images inside the boxes.

blom

paste

kos

paste

vier

paste

padda

paste

Name: _______________________ Date: _______________

Today is:

Monday | Tuesday | Wednesday

Thursday | Friday

Direction: Read, trace, and write the words.

| 1 | 2 | 3 | 4 |

no. ____	pret
no. ____	meisie
no. ____	gaan
no. ____	bok

Name : _______________________________

Trace the words. Cut out the images at the bottom. Match the words with the images by pasting the images inside the boxes.

groen

paste

ham

paste

hoed

paste

hart

paste

Name: ___________________ Date: ___________

Today is:

Monday Tuesday Wednesday

Thursday Friday

Direction: Read, trace, and write the words.

| 1 | 2 | 3 | 4 |

no. _____   huis

no. _____   perd

no. _____   ys

no. _____   roomys

Name: _________________________ Date: _______________

Today is:

| Monday | Tuesday | Wednesday |

| Thursday | Friday |

Direction: Read, trace, and write the words.

| 1  | 2  | 3  | 4  |

no. _____   konfyt

no. _____   beker

no. _____   sap

no. _____   kind

Name: _________________________   Date: _________________

Today is:

Direction: Read, trace, and write the words.

| 1 | 2 | 3 | 4 |

| no. ____ | soen |

| no. ____ | leeu |

| no. ____ | kyk |

| no. ____ | tiefde |

Name : _______________________

Direction: Match each word to the right picture. Practice writing the word.

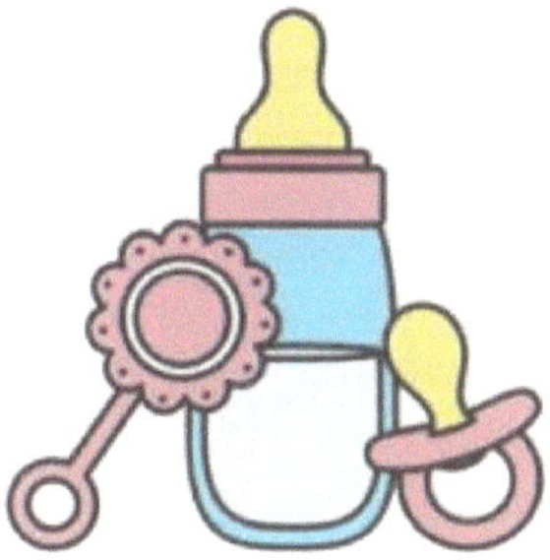

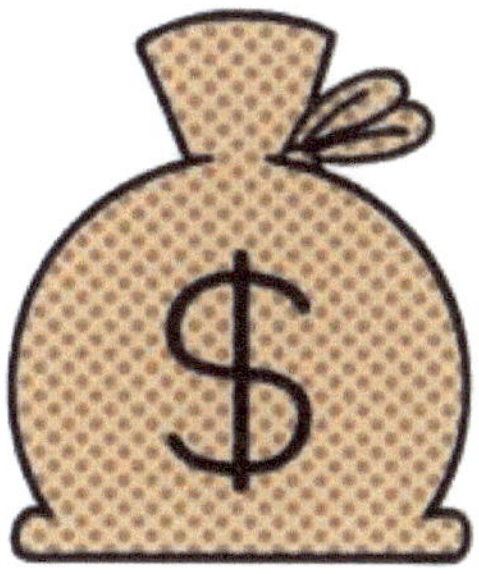

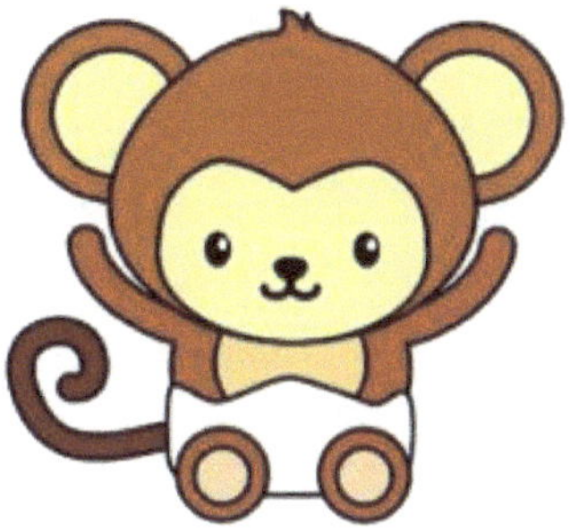

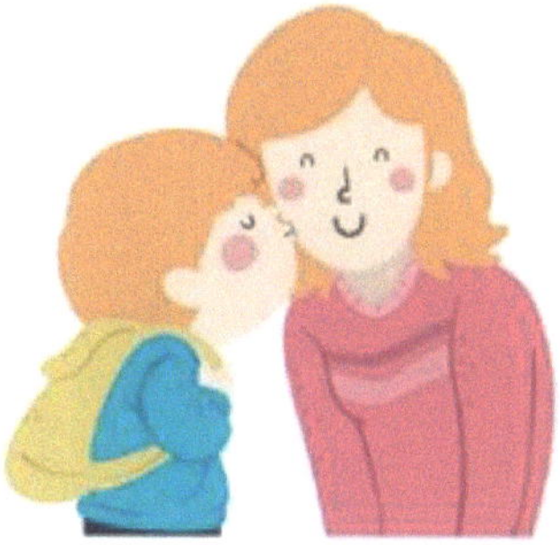

mamma

melk

geld

aap

Name : ___________________________

Read, trace, and write the words. Match the images with the traced words by writing the number that is shown on top of each image with the correct word.

rot

rot

Number ___________

maan

maan

Number ___________

nes

nes

Number ___________

nege

nege

Number ___________

1	2	3	4

Name: _______________________ Date: _______________________

Today is: Monday | Tuesday | Wednesday | Thursday | Friday

Direction: Read, trace, and write the words.

| 1 | 2 | 3 | 4 |

no. ____ neus

no. ____ een

no. ____ oranje

no. ____ uil

Name : _______________________

Read, trace, and write the words. Match the images with the traced words by writing the number that is shown on top of each image with the correct word.

verf

verf

Number _______________

pikkewyn

pikkewyn

Number _______________

vark

vark

Number _______________

pienk

pienk

Number _______________

1

2

3

4

Read, trace, and write the words. Match the images with the traced words by writing the number that is shown on top of each image with the correct word.

trek

trek

Number _______________

pot

pot

Number _______________

plante

plante

Number _______________

pers

pers

Number _______________

Name : ___________________________________

Read, trace, and write the words. Match the images with the traced words by writing the number that is shown on top of each image with the correct word.

koningin

Number _______________

vraag

Number _______________

haas

Number _______________

reën

Number _______________

| 1 | 2 | 3 | 4 |

Name : _______________________________

Read, trace, and write the words. Match the images with the traced words by writing the number that is shown on top of each image with the correct word.

sien sien Number _______	**run** run Number _______
hartseer hartseer Number _______	**rooi** rooi Number _______

1 2 3 4

Direction: Match each word to the right picture. Practice writing the word.

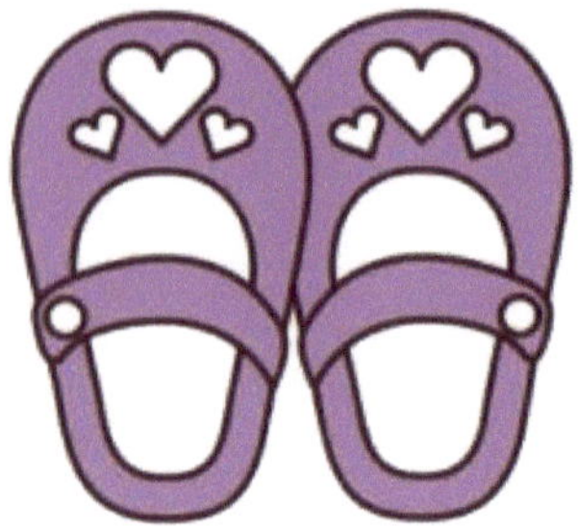

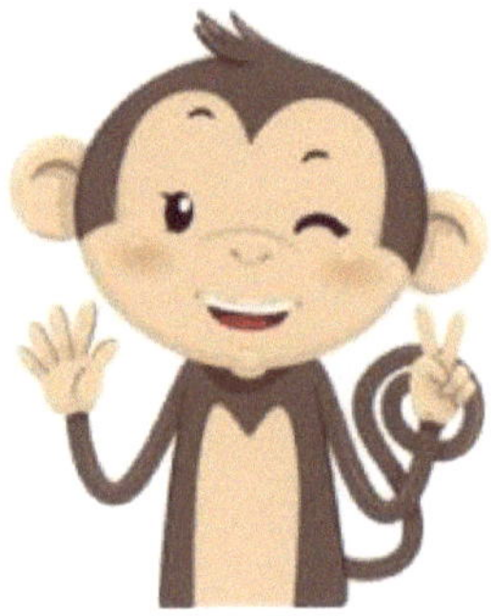

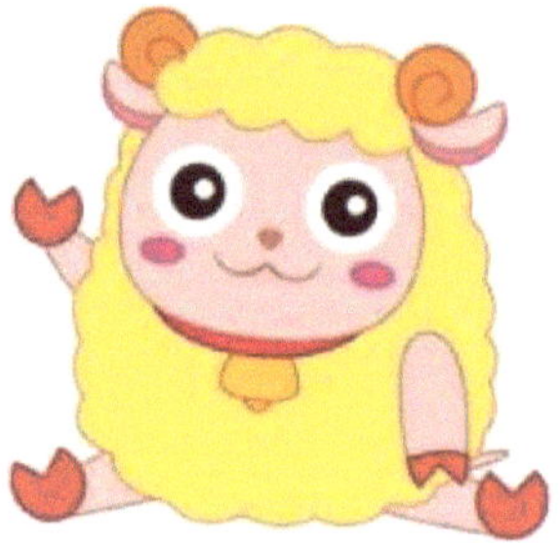

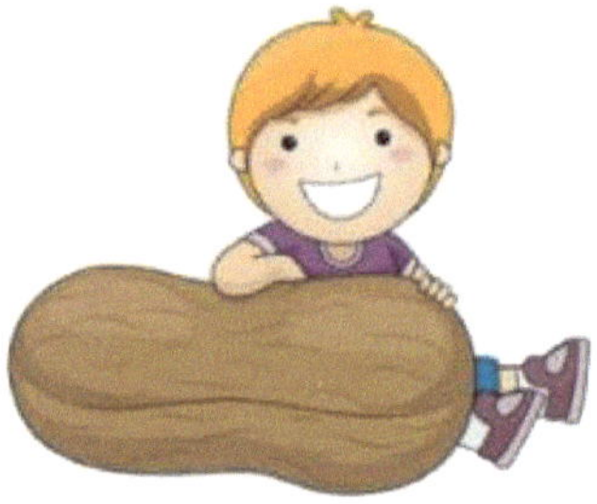

Name : _______________________________

Read, trace, and write the words. Match the images with the traced words by writing the number that is shown on top of each image with the correct word.

slaap

slaap

Number _______________

ses

ses

Number _______________

sokkie

sokkie

Number _______________

lepel

lepel

Number _______________

Name : ________________________

Read, trace, and write the words. Match the images with the traced words by writing the number that is shown on top of each image with the correct word.

<table>
<tr><td>

son

son

Number ____________

</td><td>

ster

ster

Number ____________

</td></tr>
<tr><td>

tien

tien

Number ____________

</td><td>

drie

drie

Number ____________

</td></tr>
</table>

1	2	3	4

Name : _______________________________

Trace the words. Cut out the images at the bottom. Match the words with the images by pasting the images inside the boxes.

tier

paste

speelding

paste

trein

paste

bad

paste

Direction: Match each word to the right picture. Practice writing the word.

boom

skilpad

twee

sambreel

Name : _______________________

Direction: Match each word to the right picture. Practice writing the word.

onder

van

vaas

groente

Name : _______________________________

Read, trace, and write the words. Match the images with the traced words by writing the number that is shown on top of each image with the correct word.

<table>
<tr><td>

vulkaan

vulkaan

Number ___________

</td><td>

water

water

Number ___________

</td></tr>
<tr><td>

wit

wit

Number ___________

</td><td>

venster

venster

Number ___________

</td></tr>
</table>

| 1 | 2 | 3 | 4 |

Name: _________________________ Date: _________________________

Today is: Monday   Tuesday   Wednesday   Thursday   Friday

Direction: Read, trace, and write the words.

| 1 | 2 | 3 | 4 |

no. _____ gare

no. _____ geel

no. _____ sebras

no. _____ nul

Name : ___________________________________

Read, trace, and write the words. Match the images with the traced words by writing the number that is shown on top of each image with the correct word.

mier

mier

Number ___________

appel

appel

Number ___________

vliegtuig

vliegtuig

Number ___________

krokodil

krokodil

Number ___________

1

2

3

4

Name: ____________________ Date: ____________________

Today is: Monday Tuesday Wednesday Thursday Friday

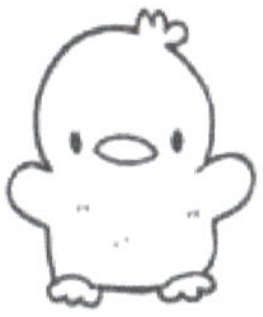

Direction: Read, trace, and write the words.

1	2	3	4
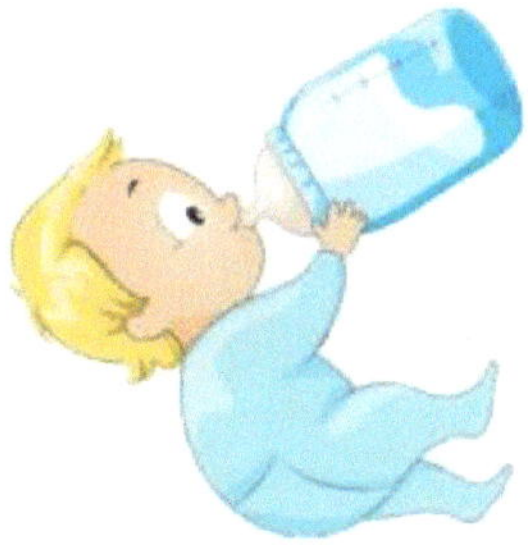	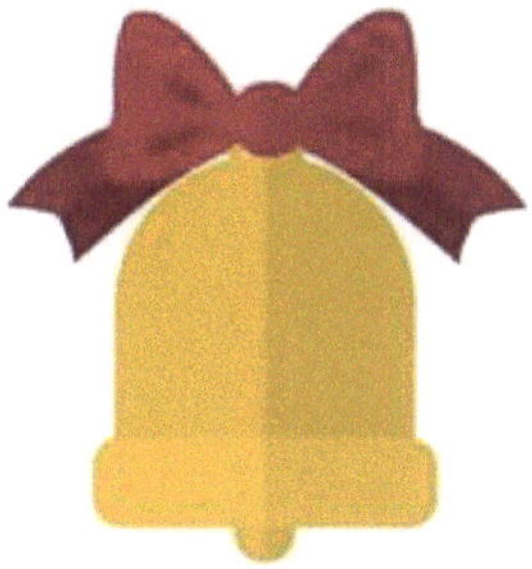	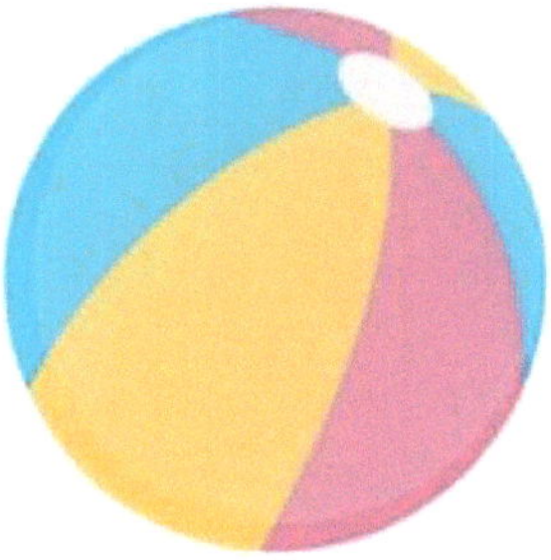	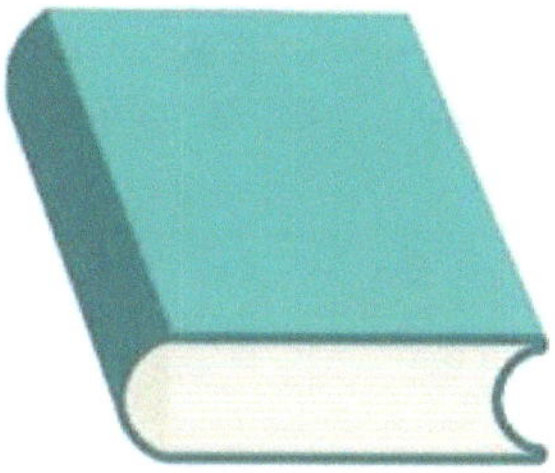

no. ____ bal

no. ____ boek

no. ____ klok

no. ____ baba

Name : _______________________________

Read, trace, and write the words. Match the images with the traced words by writing the number that is shown on top of each image with the correct word.

kat

kat

Number _______________

koring

koring

Number _______________

koei

koei

Number _______________

koek

koek

Number _______________

Name : _______________________

Trace the words. Cut out the images at the bottom. Match the words with the images by pasting the images inside the boxes.

hond

paste

pop

paste

gereg

paste

takbokke

paste

Name : ______________________________

Read, trace, and write the words. Match the images with the traced words by writing the number that is shown on top of each image with the correct word.

eier

eier

Number ____________

olifant

olifant

Number ____________

agt

agt

Number ____________

aarde

aarde

Number ____________

1	2	3	4

Name :

Direction: Match each word to the right picture. Practice writing the word.

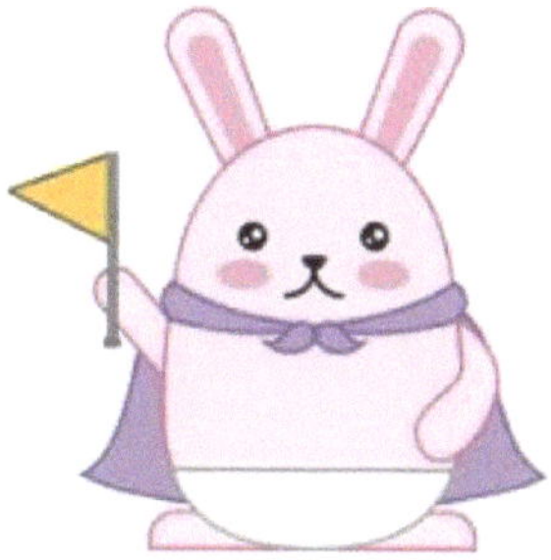 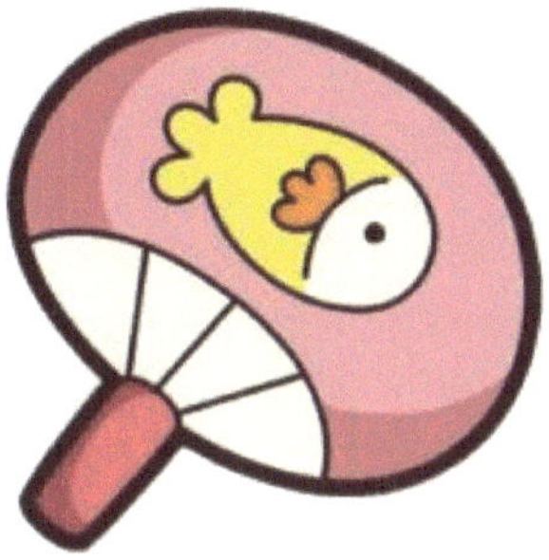 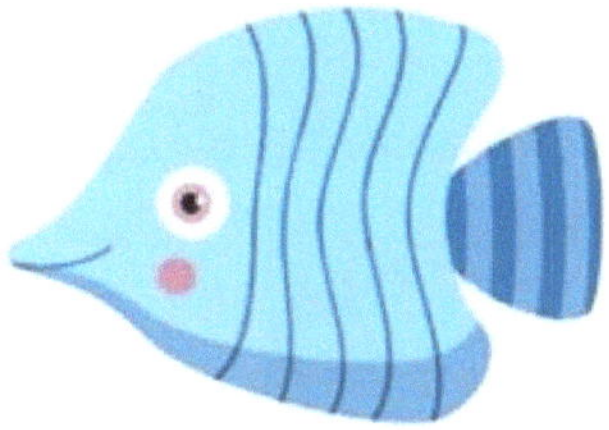 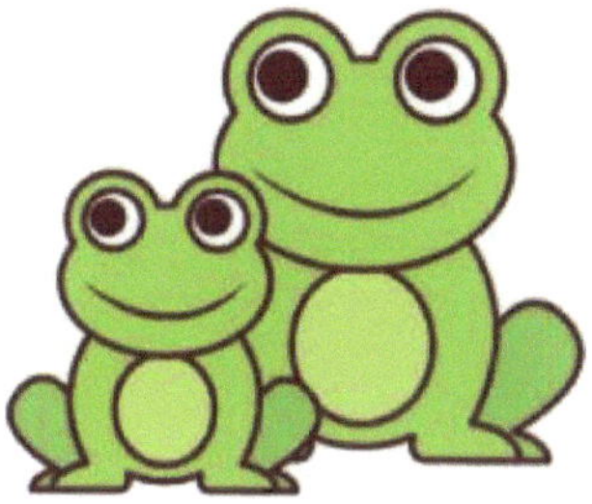

vis

padda

vlag

'n bewonderaar

Spelling Made Easy....

Name: _________________________ Date: _________________

Today is:

Direction: Read, trace, and write the words.

| 1 | 2 | 3 | 4 |

no. ____   bok

no. ____   geweer

no. ____   geskenke

no. ____   druiwe

Name: ___________________   Date: ___________

Today is:

Direction: Read, trace, and write the words.

| 1 | 2 | 3 | 4 |

no. ____   hoed

no. ____   huis

no. ____   ham

no. ____   hart